Let's Get Ready for Kwanzaa

By Joanne Winne

Children's Press
A Division of Scholastic Inc.
New York / Toronto / London / Auckland / Sydney
Mexico City / New Delhi / Hong Kong
Danbury, Connecticut

Photo Credits: Cover and all photos by Maura Boruchow
Contributing Editor: Jennifer Silate
Book Design: Victoria Johnson

Visit Children's Press on the Internet at:
http://publishing.grolier.com

Library of Congress Cataloging-in-Publication Data

Winne, Joanne.
Let's get ready for Kwanzaa / by Joanne Winne.
    p. cm. -- (Celebrations)
Includes index.
ISBN 0-516-23175-8 (lib. bdg.) -- ISBN 0-516-29571-3 (pbk.)
1. Kwanzaa--Juvenile literature. 2. African Americans--Social life and customs--
Juvenile literature. [1. Kwanzaa. 2. African Americans--Social life and customs.
3.Holidays.] I. Title.

GT4403 .W596 2001
394.261--dc21

                                                    2001017269

Contents

Look at the **calendar**.

Today is December 26.

5

It is time for **Kwanzaa**.

Kwanzaa **celebrates** our African **culture**.

BEAUFORD DELANEY '46

7

We celebrate Kwanzaa for seven days.

Friends come over to help us celebrate.

This is a **kinara**.

It holds seven **candles**.

A black candle is in the center of the kinara.

It is the first candle to be lit.

The black candle stands for the African people.

Dad places ears of corn on a straw mat.

There is one for each child in our family.

We have a **feast** on December 31.

There are many kinds of food to eat.

We play music and sing.

I like to dance.

19

The last day of Kwanzaa is January 1.

We give each other **handmade** gifts.

21

New Words

calendar **(kal**-uhn-duhr) a chart showing months, weeks, and days of the year

candles **(kan**-dls) sticks of wax with string through the center that may be burned for light

celebrates **(sehl**-uh-brayts) to honor by doing a special activity on a special day

culture **(kuhl**-chuhr) a way of living

feast **(feest)** a big meal

handmade **(hand**-mayd) something that someone makes by hand

kinara (kee-**nar**-uh) the candle holder used to celebrate Kwanzaa

Kwanzaa **(kwahn**-zuh) an African-American celebration that lasts seven days

To Find Out More

Books
K is for Kwanzaa: A Kwanzaa Alphabet Book
by Juwanda G. Ford
Scholastic

The Gifts of Kwanzaa
by Synthia S. James
Albert Whitman & Company

Web Site
Afro-Americ@: Kids Zone
http://www.afroam.org/children/fun/kwanzaa/kwanzaa.html
Learn all about Kwanzaa on this Web site.

Index

About the Author

Joanne Winne taught fourth grade for nine years. She currently writes and edits books for children. She lives in Hoboken, New Jersey.

Reading Consultants

Kris Flynn, Coordinator, Small School District Literacy, The San Diego County Office of Education

Shelly Forys, Certified Reading Recovery Specialist, W.J. Zahnow Elementary School, Waterloo, IL

Sue McAdams, Former President of the North Texas Reading Council of the IRA, and Early Literacy Consultant, Dallas, TX

m